MARIJUANA

EVE AND
ALBERT
STWERTKA

MARIJUANA

A FIRST BOOK | REVISED EDITION
NEW YORK | LONDON | TORONTO | SYDNEY
FRANKLIN WATTS | 1986

Photographs courtesy of:
Drug Enforcement Administration: p. 3;
UPI/Bettmann Newsphotos: pp. 6, 18, 34, 53;
New York Public Library: p. 13;
AP/Wide World: pp. 21, 28, 43, 56.

Library of Congress Cataloging in Publication Data

Stwertka, Eve.
Marijuana.
(A First book)
Bibliography: p.
Includes index.
Summary: A general history of marijuana use
including its source, ways of consumption, side effects,
continuing popularity, and the debate over its
decriminalization.
1. Marihuana—Juvenile literature. [1. Marihuana]
I. Stwertka, Albert. II. Title.
HV5822.M3S88   1986   613.8'3   85-22526
ISBN 0-531-10122-3   (rev.)

CONTENTS

MARIJUANA

INTRODUCTION

It's hard to imagine that before the 1950s many Americans had never even heard of marijuana. It meant nothing to most young people in schools and it was seldom in the news.

By the 1980s, though, sixty million Americans—a quarter of our population—acknowledged having used marijuana. In a confidential poll of high school students around the country, nearly a third said they had tried it, and a 1984 survey in New York State found that many children had experimented with marijuana even before seventh grade.

What is this illegal substance? What does it do to users' minds and bodies? And what causes people to break the law for it and to risk its harmful effects?

A MIND-ALTERING PLANT

The plants we find in nature affect our bodies in many different ways. Some give us nourishment, others cure us when we are ill. Still others are poisonous and can even kill us.

There are also plants that have a startling effect on the mind. This happens because the substances they contain act on the user's brain and nervous system. One plant containing such mind-altering, or psychoactive, substances is marijuana, also known as hemp or cannabis.

In recent years there has been a great deal of public debate about the use of marijuana as a mind-altering drug.

Governments in many parts of the world have declared it dangerous and have made selling or using it illegal. Because smoking or eating parts of this plant makes people feel and act rather strangely, legislators assumed that its effects must be harmful. Scientific experiments of the last few years show that this is indeed so. On the other hand, however, there are many people who like to celebrate moments of free time by getting "high," or tipsy. Throughout the centuries, people have used beer, wine, or stronger alcoholic drinks to help them relax and enjoy sociable occasions. Tobacco, too, has been used for this purpose.

Today we know that alcohol and tobacco damage people's bodies and minds when used regularly or in large quantities. Yet, because these substances are part of an old tradition, the right to use them is only slightly restricted by laws.

Is marijuana more harmful than tobacco and alcohol? Our legislators have long thought so. Now scientists are doing research to bring us the facts. When a drug is new to the people using it, they can easily make mistakes about its effects. For example, heroin, a truly dangerous narcotic drug, was praised, at first, as a harmless cure for morphine addiction. Not many years ago, several medications were prescribed as perfectly safe for women expecting babies. Later, the remedies were found to have caused birth defects in these women's children.

It takes at least twenty years for the tumor-producing effects of cigarette smoking to appear. As for marijuana, it hasn't been in steady use long enough, in our society, for all possible results to have been observed. You can see, then, how important it is to study all possible effects of this drug on human bodies and minds.

Even though the marijuana plant is thousands of years old, Western civilization has never before had much use for its mind-altering powers. Most Europeans and Americans

A crop of hemp, known botanically as Cannabis sativa, *or marijuana*

knew it only as an ordinary farm crop called hemp. It was grown for making clothing, rope, paper, varnish, and bird food.

In the last fifty years, though, the marijuana habit slowly moved north and west from southern regions of the world, where mood-changing substances in the plant have always been stronger.

The marijuana plant is used for several different purposes. Even as a drug or "dope" it is consumed in various ways. It can be smoked, drunk, or eaten. Some forms of it are mild, others very potent. It has dozens of different nicknames, such as "grass," "tea," and "pot." It even has several other spellings. "Marijuana" is the spelling most often seen in America and England. United States government publications, though, use "marihuana," and some dictionaries also consider "marahuana" acceptable. All these are different forms of the Mexican-Spanish *mariguana.*

Experts like to avoid confusion by using the scientific name "cannabis" when they talk about the marijuana plant and its products. This name was coined by the eighteenth-century Swedish botanist Linnaeus. In his listing of the plant world, he called hemp or marijuana *Cannabis sativa* —Latin for "canelike" and "cultivated." The general word "cannabis" includes all forms of the plant, as well as the drugs made from its leaves and flowers.

THE PLANT
CALLED
CANNABIS

Cannabis sativa, or hemp, or marijuana, is a tall, green, strong-smelling plant. It grows as a hardy weed or cultivated crop in temperate climates everywhere.

Throughout the ages, people have woven the fibrous tissue of the hemp stalk into clothing, rope, and paper. They have pressed the hemp seeds to make oil for paints and varnish, and dried the seeds as food for canaries and other songbirds. However, they also discovered that the leaves and flowers of cannabis, especially in very warm climates, contain mysterious compounds that have a mood-changing effect on the human brain.

The variety of hemp that is specially grown for its fibrous tissue can reach a height of 18 feet (5.5 m). The tissues run under the bark of the long hollow stem. Because the stem is the most important part of this variety, it has few side branches, and they are spare and narrow.

The drug-producing strains of cannabis flourish best in climates that are hot and dry. They grow mainly in India, the Arab countries, northern Africa, South America, and Mexico. These plants have short stems and many wide branches, thick with leaves and flowers. A recently developed hybrid strain grows well in North America.

Cannabis is an annual plant. It sprouts from a seed in the spring. In the summer it flowers and produces new seeds, and at the end of the season it dies. There is also a new variety that is seedless and very potent. It is propagated from cuttings. The leaves of marijuana are lightly

(5)

The leaves of marijuana are lightly haired,
with pointed tips and saw-toothed edges.

haired, with pointed tips and saw-toothed edges. The lower sets of leaves grow opposite each other, but the upper leaves alternate from side to side. This gives the plant a tumbled, windblown look.

MALES AND FEMALES

You may be surprised to read that each cannabis plant is either male or female. Only rarely—in climates where the days are short—do some plants carry both male and female blooms. Plants whose reproductive system is separated in this way are called dioecious. Winds carry pollen from the reproductive parts of the male plants to the blossom pistils of the female plants, where the seeds are produced.

When a cannabis crop is about four months old, half the plants look taller and narrower than the others. These are the males. Above their leaves they carry small, pale, green and purple blossoms. A week or two later, the female plants also begin to blossom. Whitish flowers appear on pairs of spikes that are carried on the upper leaves. The pistil of each flower is surrounded by a small curved leaf called a bract. The inside of the bract is lined with glands and small hairs that catch the pollen carried by the wind. High mid-summer heat causes the glands in the bract to secrete strong-smelling resin. This sticky substance protects the blossom from the heat and keeps it moist. It is this part of the plant that is highest in drug content. The hotter and drier the climate, the more powerful are the psychoactive mind-altering compounds in the blossoms and their resin.

When the wind-borne pollen joins the female flowers, fruits begin to form. The male plant has now done its part. It starts to wilt and die. At the end of the summer, the fruits of the female plant look like small, smooth, brown nuts, each containing a single seed. If the plants are not harvested, they die with the first frost. Only the seed inside the hard-shelled nut survives.

Marijuana growers have little use for the male plants. Usually the grower uproots them as soon as they can be recognized and takes them away before their pollen can fertilize the female plant. It has long been believed that the female produces more drug-laden resin when its energies are not taken up with nourishing the seed fruit. Recently, though, this belief has been questioned by scientists.

The new seedless strain of cannabis is called "sinsemilla"—Spanish for "without seeds." Its drug-laden buds contain a concentrate of potent chemicals because the plant's energies are not taken up with nourishing seed-fruits. In fact, its psychoactive components are thought to be ten times more powerful than those formerly obtainable from plants grown in Mexico and Colombia.

CURING

Careful growers pick each part of the female plant separately—the resin-rich blossoms, the upper leaves, and the comparatively resin-poor lower leaves. Proper curing, or drying, is needed to develop the desired chemicals.

In a hot, dry climate the best curing is done outdoors. To cure the crop, growers hang it upside down on racks or branches. After a few days they enclose bunches of leaves and flowers in paper bags. This prevents them from becoming too dry. Each day, the bags must be opened to let in fresh air, and closed again, so that no fungus can form inside. A week later, the crop is ready to be stored. It will retain its strength for about a year.

CANNABIS,
MILD AND POTENT

The shredded brown smoking mixture usually called marijuana consists of dried hemp flowers, upper and lower leaves, and small stems.

(8)

Before smoking this mixture, users usually have to clean it by discarding the stems and seeds. Otherwise the sharp little stems poke holes in the cigarette-rolling paper, and the seeds explode when they catch fire.

Marijuana is the mildest form of cannabis. Depending on growing conditions and the proportion of leaves to flowers, it contains between 0 and 3 percent of the psychoactive substance delta-9 tetrahydrocannabinol (delta-9 THC). In India, this mild form of the weed is named bhang.

The strongest drug of the cannabis plant is made from the resin of the female flowers. It is called hashish or, in India and other Far Eastern countries, charas. It is produced chiefly in the hot, dry climates of Nepal, Afghanistan, Lebanon, and Morocco.

To separate the resin from the blossoms, many growers still use a primitive method. They beat the flowering tops against a rough material such as burlap. Lumps form and are scraped off. Usually, the thick, brown, smelly mass is then mixed with sugar to add weight.

Even more concentrated than solid hashish is an extract known as hashish oil. It is a black, tarlike liquid made by "percolating" cannabis flowers and leaves through a fatty solvent.

Hashish is highly intoxicating. While uncultivated marijuana is not likely to contain more than 3 percent of the mind-altering drug delta-9 THC, hashish may contain between 10 and 15 percent and hashish oil anywhere from 20 to 65 percent.

SURVIVAL SKILL

Because of its hairy leaves and strong smell, cannabis has few natural enemies. Except for extreme cold, every climate suits cannabis and its tough-shelled seeds. That is why it grows wild, even in the backyards and empty areas of cities. It is truly one of the hardiest weeds in existence.

HOW OLD
IS THE
MARIJUANA
HABIT?

Historians tend to agree that cultivation of hemp started in China thousands of years ago and slowly moved westward throughout the centuries.

The ancient Chinese grew vast quantities of the fibrous stalks for weaving cloth. They had little regard, though, for the plant's mind-altering effects. Chinese social life was strict and mannerly. Certain effects of cannabis—sudden laughter, rambling talk, voracious hunger, reddened eyes—could only meet with disapproval in such a culture. Hemp juice was therefore called the "liberator of sin."

Yet, the learned Emperor Shen-Nung mentions hemp in his pharmacy book, written about 2657 B.C. He recommends it as a cure for "gout, rheumatism, malaria, beriberi, constipation, and absentmindedness."

Folk custom of ancient China used the supposed magic in hemp for a more indirect cure. Country people carved the stalk of the plant in the shape of a snake's head. When someone was ill, the relatives beat the patient's bed with this stalk to drive the illness away.

Many centuries later, in the Chou period (about 221 to 100 B.C.), the pleasant feelings brought on by hemp juice were sometimes used for "enjoyment of life," and a Chinese work of the fourth century A.D. mentions that drinking this juice makes one see spirits.

In the third century A.D., Hoa-Tho, a Chinese physician, had his patients drink a mixture of cannabis resin and wine before they underwent surgery. It seems to have worked as an anesthetic, for he reports in his autobiography that his patients felt no pain.

MYSTERY AND DARING: ANCIENT INDIA

In China, hemp was grown chiefly for its fibrous stalk. In India, though, it was grown for the resinous juice of the female flower and its psychoactive powers.

An Indian legend has it that the god Shiva brought the hemp plant from the Himalaya Mountains and gave it to humanity. Indian culture inclined people to mystery. The wise person, it was thought, keeps aloof from coarse reality and holds the world at some distance. The juice of marijuana helped people to withdraw from daily cares. Not only religious mystics but people in all walks of life used mild preparations of cannabis, or bhang.

The most popular form of bhang was a drink brewed from cannabis leaves and milk and sweetened with sugar. Also popular was a sweetmeat called majoom, made of cannabis, sugar, milk, flour, and butter.

In Indian legends, heroes would perform feats of daring after drinking bhang. Bhang was prescribed for young girls to help them eat with a better appetite. It was also drunk on religious holidays, and students of religion and holy men took it before meditation and ceremonies.

Yet even in India there were mixed feelings about the marijuana habit. A collection of folk tales, *The Mahbharata*, states that a person who wishes to become successful should avoid several fruits as well as the leaves of bhang.

When Christian missionaries came to India in the nineteenth century, they criticized the religious meaning attached to bhang. To the missionaries, the Indians' religious trance appeared to be nothing more than the effect of dope.

In the 1950s the economic life of India seemed to have become stagnant. Little progress had occurred for centuries, and it was thought that drug habits had misled people into giving up trying to improve their social conditions. A drug study was undertaken, and the results were reported to the League of Nations. The study concluded that cannabis was so much a part of Indian life that it would not be practical to pass laws against it. More recently, though, India's legislators joined those of other nations in condemning the use of marijuana.

SMOKE AND VAPOR:
THE WESTWARD TRAIL

It is possible to pick up the trail of cannabis use as it spread westward. In Book IV of Homer's *Odyssey*, the famous Helen of Troy served her guest a drug which "melted sorrow and . . . made men forgetful of their pains." Since the drug is said to have come from the "ploughlands of Egypt," it might have been marijuana.

Somewhat later, a Greek historian of the fifth century B.C. described a custom of the Scythian people. They would throw hemp seeds and leaves on red-hot stones and breathe in the pungent fumes. As a result they became drunk, and danced, sang, and screamed.

The communal method of inhaling the fumes was used from the thirteenth century A.D. on, by a few tribes in northern and central Africa. Later, these tribes developed a way to suck in the smoke through long hollow tubes. If the drug was strong and the smoke harsh to the throat, they passed it across a coconut or gourd full of cooling water. Still later, in Middle Eastern countries, this became the way to smoke the concentrated cannabis resin, hashish. Hashish pipes come equipped with a water bottle and a long, coiled flexible tube, to cool the smoke before it reached the mouthpiece.

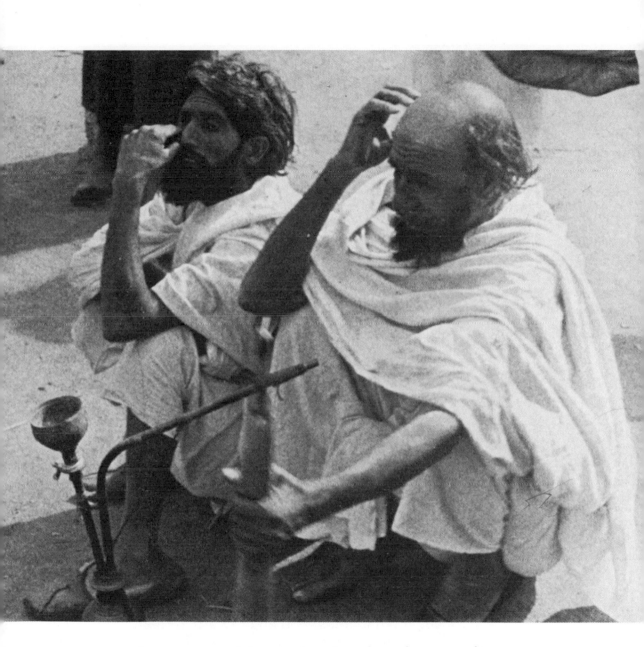

In some countries, water pipes have been used to smoke hashish, a concentrated form of cannabis.

LAUGHING LEAVES
AND HAPPY SEEDS

Most early Greek and Roman writers mention cannabis only in passing. They treat it as a curious rarity. The naturalist writer Pliny (first century A.D.) mentions a plant he calls *gellotophyllis*, or "laughing leaf." The Greek physician Galen (A.D. 130 to 193), who was interested in the science of drugs, remarks on certain small cakes that were offered to guests at parties. They may have been cannabis cakes, for they made people laugh and feel excited, hungry, thirsty, and finally sluggish.

The ancient Greeks and Romans celebrated their festivities with wine. They were not inclined to make a habit of marijuana. On the whole, they saw the plant as a medical herb for the treatment of intestinal pains, swellings, earache, headache, and many other complaints. This, too, is the way the drug was prescribed by Arab physicians throughout the Middle Ages.

ASSASSINATION
AND DISORDER

Well before the year 1000, the concentrated marijuana resin called hashish was known and somewhat feared in Arab countries. From the word *hashishin*, "a hemp eater," comes the word "assassin," or " murderer." The fairy tales of *The Arabian Nights* tell of reckless deeds committed by people who abused the drug. Perhaps these tales even served to advertise hashish, tempting others to try it.

The legend of an eleventh-century Arab outlaw, Hasan-Ibn-Sabbah, reinforces the bad reputation of hashish. It seems that Hasan was followed by a personal army of cutthroats. He collected jobless men and rewarded them with a supply of hashish. In return, he expected them to obey his orders to kill and plunder.

The theory that hashish makes users violent seems to begin earlier, though, with the legends of old India, whose warriors drank bhang before going into battle. The fact is that in some people the drug reduces fears and anxiety. It enables them to disregard danger. Then, after the effects of the drug have worn off, steady users may tend to be irritable and short-tempered.

The violence of outlaw bands, made bolder by cannabis, has often been feared by peaceful citizens. What many governments fear even more is the tendency of dope takers to become idle and unable to take care of themselves. In recent years, countries such as Egypt and Nigeria, wishing to improve their general living conditions, have taken a strong stand against cannabis products. In 1960 an official Egyptian government publication stated that cannabis is "of no value whatever to humanity and deserving of nothing but the contempt of civilized people."

CENTRAL EUROPE

Early peoples of central Europe used flax rather than hemp strands for weaving cloth. Therefore cannabis was little known until wayfarers brought some of it back to France from northern Africa in the nineteenth century. Soon, a small group of hashish eaters, many of them artists and writers, held regular meetings in a fashionable Paris hotel. They called themselves the Club of the Hachichiens. The way they wrote about their drugged visions introduced their habit to the world as an exciting new pastime.

THE NEW WORLD

In the days of the American colonies, when sailing ships required vast lengths of stout rope, acres of hemp were grown in America. In the eighteenth century, most of the settlers' clothes were made of hemp. George Washington mentions in his diaries that he grew hemp on his plantation. We have no evidence, though, that during those years Americans ate or smoked parts of the plant. Probably, the fibrous kind of hemp they grew in a relatively cool climate simply did not produce much psychoactive material. Later, cotton was introduced as a fibrous crop and took the place of hemp. When the days of sailing ships were over, hemp was abandoned. The plant continued to grow as a weed but received little notice.

Farther south, though, under the burning Mexican skies, marijuana was rich in mind-altering chemicals. The Aztecs had long used cannabis in religious ceremonies. In Mexico the plant grew freely and was obtainable by everyone. The poor people of Mexico often smoked it to give themselves relief from a drab existence.

During World War I, Mexican workers began to go across the U.S. border for the fruit-picking season. They were used to carrying little tobacco pouches of dried cannabis. Now and then they would take a smoke to give themselves a lift during the hard day's work.

At about the same time, sailors from Jamaica and other Caribbean ports came to the docks of New Orleans. They knew marijuana by its Hindu name, ganja, because its use had been introduced to the West Indies by indentured workers brought over from India. The Jamaican sailors carried their own supply of ganja and shared it with their new companions. Slowly the use of cannabis spread along the shipping route of the Mississippi River.

Soon, the free-growing weed was no longer considered good enough. Smokers demanded a purified product with a higher drug content. Marijuana was imported from Cuba as well as from Mexico. As a result, the prices doubled several times during the 1920s. Importers quickly took advantage of the fact that there was money to be made on the drug.

For the first time, newspapers began to feature stories connecting marijuana with crime. They reported that it was used by idlers, drifters, and vicious characters. Dope sellers were said to wait outside school yards selling marijuana cigarettes, or "muggles," cheaply to schoolchildren. The air of excitement these newspaper stories created served to advertise the drug. It tempted others to try it, drove up the price, and gave it added importance.

By 1937 marijuana was outlawed everywhere in the United States, even though its use had remained limited to small, scattered groups. For some years, America had been in an economic depression. Incomes were close to the margin of necessity. There wasn't much celebrating going on and drugs were the last thing people wanted to buy. When the United States entered the Second World War, economic austerity continued.

The end of the war, however, brought plenty of jobs and money. Americans went on a spending spree. Among other things, they bought portable radios and record players and sent the record industry booming. From the early days of jazz, musicians had occasionally smoked marijuana during their "jam sessions." Now, young rock groups working in the jazz tradition started to copy the habit. Some thought "grass" might help to inspire the creation of their complex, inventive music.

Rock and roll reached the public just as the kids of the postwar baby boom reached their teens. The result was instant recognition. The two were made for each other. Rock groups proliferated. Youngsters bought stereos and maximized the volume. They stockpiled albums, swarmed to concerts and festivals, read all about their rock star idols, and tried to imitate them in all things. Pot smoking, though

illegal, became a familiar aspect of the rock scene, and many song lyrics dealt with marijuana and other drugs. To understand these lyrics was to be a member of a secret society. Thus, in the public mind, drugs became associated with youth and rebellion.

The 1960s were also a time of civil liberation in the United States, when minorities gained the power to change many outdated laws. Their victories strengthened a sense that laws can be confining and unjust. As a result, many people developed the notion that laws which could not be changed could simply be disregarded. Some of these men and women paid a high price for this attitude by being arrested and having to carry a criminal record for the rest of their lives.

Finally, thousands of young Americans went to war in Vietnam. There, cannabis and other drugs were easily available. Often, soldiers turned to marijuana for relief from the misery of war. When they returned home, they continued the habit.

Today, the association of marijuana with music and college youth is only a faded memory. Drug users are to be found in every age group and social class, and marijuana has been commercially developed into a more potent and expensive drug. It has become a billion-dollar business. Increasingly, it is now used together with alcohol and other drugs, which makes it far more damaging. Who could have predicted that the marijuana habit, so recent in America, would become widespread within a few decades?

"Taking a hit" at a Miami Beach
"smoke in" in the early 1970s

THE
POT USER'S
WORLD

To use marijuana is not only unlawful; it is expensive. In spite of this, sixty million Americans are estimated to have tried it at least once. There is more than one reason why so many people do something that is illegal, costly, and harmful.

Evidently, some people try pot out of sheer curiosity or to be in on something "new." Others find childlike excitement in a secret, forbidden activity. Still others are looking for a drug to give them a few moments of feeling high and at peace with the world. Finally, for many people with time on their hands, marijuana provides an opportunity to experiment. It can also be a lively subject of conversation.

HEAD SHOPS

The selling and buying of cannabis is forbidden, but strangely enough, the selling and buying of related objects is not. At so-called head shops in many cities, and through mail-order directories, those who are interested can buy all sorts of items of marijuana gadgetry. Among these are weighing scales, sifters, rolling papers, clay pipes and water pipes, cigarette holders, storage jars, and instruction booklets. Marijuana fanciers can read magazines devoted to nothing but cannabis news. Home cooks can even buy marijuana recipe books, listing such oddities as pot burgers and cannabis beans, grass pizza and hashish brownies. As

At so-called head shops, those who are interested
can buy all sorts of marijuana gadgetry.

you can see, for many people marijuana has become a kind of undercover hobby.

Some 30,000 head shops are estimated to exist in the United States, and yearly sales are thought to run into $1.5 billion.

For years, now, parent groups, townships, and even state legislatures have tried to ban the sale of drug-related items. Store owners, though, have resisted all attempts to close them down. Represented by their own national trade organization, the head shops argue that any law to oust them is unconstitutional.

Most legal authorities agree that under the Constitution it is indeed difficult to make such a law stick. The store owners have one standard answer when asked about the matter: "I just sell it. I don't ask my customers what they use these things for, and my customers don't tell me."

OCCASIONAL USERS

Marijuana smoking is often a social activity. The occasion might be a party, where someone will roll a marijuana "joint," light it, take a puff (called a "toke"), and pass it to another person. The cigarette itself is a soggy object of light shade, loosely packed, thick in the middle, and sealed with saliva. It burns down very quickly to a small brown butt. Dope-takers call this the "roach." Soaked with psycho-active compounds, the roach is considered the most potent part of the joint. Because it is small and hot, it is gripped with a special holder, or "roach clip."

EFFECTS ON THE BODY

Marijuana smokers are enthusiastic about what happens next. Within four or five minutes of inhaling the cigarette, the smoker's heart starts to beat much faster. The heart rate can increase from 80 beats a minute to 150 or so, depending on the strength of the smoke.

At the same time, the smoker's bronchial tubes—the air passages to the lungs—relax and become enlarged. Air rushes into the body's respiratory system. Partly, it is the additional oxygen that causes people to feel high.

The blood vessels in the membrane covering the eyes expand. More blood flows into the widened vessels, creating the typical red eyes of the marijuana smoker. Other blood vessels, too, become dilated, causing a general drop in blood pressure. Because of this low blood pressure, less blood is able to flow to the brain and a feeling of dizziness results.

Smokers' muscular coordination and body balance are slightly impaired, and their hands may tremble and become unsteady. Occasionally, their hands and feet are cold and their general body temperature drops.

EFFECTS ON THE MIND

When the drug enters a user's bloodstream, it soon reaches the deeper parts of the brain. Here it causes changes in the area that collects information coming in from all the senses —sight, hearing, touch, taste, and smell. This is also the area that controls the person's mood. As a result, his or her perceptions and sense of reality become distorted. Often, users suddenly feel pleasant emotions. Hues and sounds seem to them more intense. Even the touch of an ordinary drinking glass may be a new experience. Time appears to have slowed down to infinity. The user's mouth feels dry, and he or she is hungry and thirsty. In drug slang, this is called feeling "the munchies."

Depending on the strength of cannabis used, the high can be as brief as five minutes or as long as an hour. When the high wears off, smokers become sluggish, or "stoned," and are apt to go to sleep. The morning-after effects of pot are generally less unpleasant than an alcoholic hangover. Smokers are likely to feel listless but free of headache and nausea.

Occasionally people report that a few days after having used marijuana, they experience sudden psychoactive effects. What causes such "flashbacks" is not well understood. Perhaps it is due to the fact that marijuana accumulates and remains stored in the body and brain.

THE OUTSIDE VIEW

Seen by an outsider, a person high on marijuana has blood-shot eyes, talks a lot without making too much sense, and often laughs and giggles for no good reason. Movements become slow and uncertain. In the later stages of intoxication, a user becomes withdrawn and shows a stony facial expression.

Although many smokers report that cannabis sharpens all their senses, experiments have not proved this to be really so. On the contrary, recent evidence shows that the ability to drive a car, for example, becomes severely reduced. Drivers under the influence of the drug take longer to put their foot on the brake. Their reaction time in general is slower, and they have lapses of attention that could greatly affect their judgment in traffic situations. It also takes longer for their eyes to recover from glare when they drive at night.

It is not surprising that the distortions caused by cannabis affect the brain's ability to perform in other ways. Experiments have shown that under the influence of marijuana, people's ability to count and to use words deteriorates. They experience a significant drop in short-term memory, and these disabilities become more serious as the dose increases.

THE CANNABIS
"BUMMER"

Occasionally, the cannabis experience can become a nightmare. Instead of meeting with the pleasant sensations described by others, a user may think that he or she is going crazy, and feel anxious, depressed, or panicky. There are estimates that this negative reaction happens 20 percent of the time. Among new users it happens even more often. No one really knows the reason for this kind of "bad trip," or "bummer." The reaction has something to do with the personality and the mood of the user. Then, too, cannabis varies in strength and chemical composition. Some pot may be much more concentrated than expected. At times it may be poisoned by insecticides or herbicides sprayed by the grower. It may be high in mold spores that cause coughing and wheezing.

Eating a strong dose of cannabis is more likely to give one a bad trip than smoking it. Digestion is a much slower but surer way than inhaling for any substance to reach the bloodstream. When pot is smoked, the bloodstream carries it to the brain within five minutes. When pot is eaten, the process takes about an hour. In the meantime, people sometimes eat more and more, waiting for something to happen. When it finally does, it can be terrifying. The only way to help people get rid of the cannabis they have ingested is to rush them to a hospital emergency room to have the contents of their stomach pumped out.

ANGEL DUST

When people buy an illegal substance, they seldom know just what they are getting. Because the price of marijuana has risen beyond the means of many youngsters, sellers are resorting to additives. Cigarettes are frequently laced with chopped weeds, parsley, tea leaves, and cheap medication. The most destructive of these is sold on the streets under the name of "love" or "angel dust" or "T."

These pretty names disguise an ugly reality. Angel dust is the animal tranquilizer phencyclidine (PCP). After heroin and cocaine, it is the drug now most often responsible for emergency room overdose cases. PCP is rather simple and inexpensive to manufacture in an improvised chemistry laboratory. But for the one who buys it, it can spell disaster. Under the influence of PCP, users often become violent, wreck their surroundings, and threaten those near them. For example, a PCP intoxicated driver killed eight people when he crashed his vehicle into a bus stop. PCP causes severe seizures, symptoms like those of schizophrenia, and sudden relapses long after original use.

PCP is mistakenly called "T" because it is sometimes misrepresented as THC, or tetrahydrocannabinol, the most important psychoactive compound in marijuana.

HABITUAL USERS

Cannabis is not considered to be physically addictive. This means that steady users can stop their regular intake without becoming violently ill. Nevertheless, they do become psychologically dependent on the lift the drug gives them. Deprived of it, they become nervous, angry, or depressed.

The Mexicans have a song—"La Cucaracha"—about a cockroach that can't move another step because it has run out of marijuana to smoke. In American drug slang, this cockroach is "strung out."

Like most steady drug users, those regularly taking marijuana are looking for relief from anxious feelings. If they have difficulty in coping with their problems, they may turn to pot for relief from worries. The problems are not solved, but they seem less pressing. The drug may help the user not to become upset, or "uncool."

In countries where marijuana is an ancient habit, it has long been suspected that steady use makes people lose energy and ambition. Some reputable modern researchers now consider this to be a proven fact. Others, however, believe that the evidence is still too limited to permit conclusions.

There seems to be no basis for the once-popular notion that marijuana is a killer weed that drives people to crime and insanity. As early as 1898, a British study made in India put the matter this way: Heavy cannabis users were hardly ever aggressive criminals. Rather, they were passive individuals whose need for the drug at times led them to theft and other petty crimes. Usually they were poor and becoming poorer, because they turned to the drug instead of educating themselves or earning a living. Unable to support themselves and often ashamed of their condition, they might end up ill in the streets, or in the public ward of a mental hospital.

NICKELS, DIMES, AND KEYS

The pot users' world is united by a common underground language. First of all, the weed itself has a long string of names. "Marijuana"—in English, "Mary Jane"—is derived from the Spanish-Mexican word *mariguana*, a word whose origin is uncertain. The name makes one think of an attractive young woman who is good company. Other popular names such as grass, tea, and pot also suggest familiar and comfortable things. These affectionate names clearly show that, right or wrong, cannabis users consider their drug innocent and harmless.

When pot users, also known as "heads," gather to smoke, they talk about "blowing some weed" or "taking a hit." In America, an ounce (28.4 g) is called a lid (because it was formerly measured in the top of a tobacco can) or a

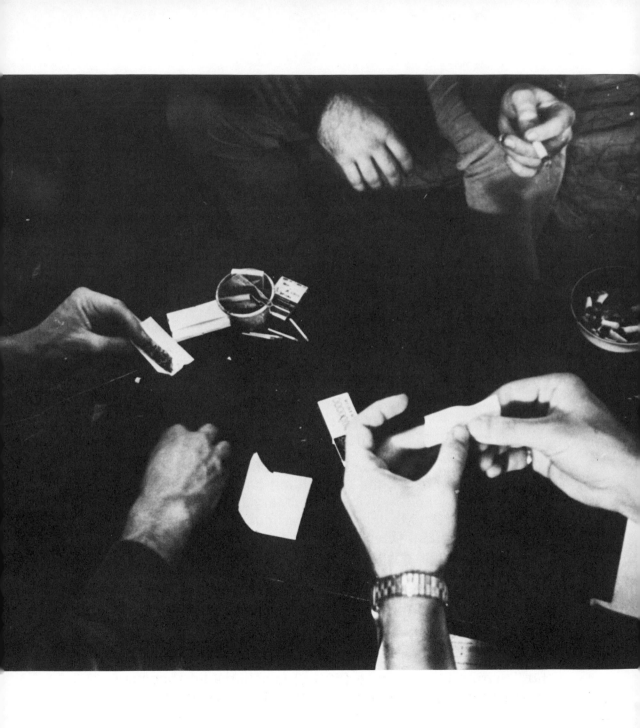

"Z"; 5 dollars' worth is a nickel bag; 10 dollars' worth is a dime; and 1 kilogram (2.2 pounds) a key.

Safely hidden away, the drug supply is called "the stash." A smoker taking too many hits is liable to get "smashed" and to "freak out." Any sudden unpleasantness can bring smokers down from their high and cause them to "crash."

Nowadays, users talk about "doing" dope or grass rather than "smoking" it. In fact, the verb *doing* has attached itself to all the different types of drug activity. This indicates a change from the early years of marijuana's underground popularity, when smokers used to look down on liquor and the more addictive drugs. The expression "doing drugs" implies that all drugs are to some extent interchangeable; and indeed, mixing drugs is becoming more widespread.

Slang words in common such as these, a common habit, and common related concerns make up what social scientists call the drug subculture.

Rolling marijuana
"joints" at a party

THE CHEMISTRY OF CANNABIS

Marijuana is a tricky plant. Its chemistry is changeable and complicated. Until recently, researchers were unable to establish the exact strength and composition of the cannabis they were using in each experiment.

Over 400 different compounds have been found in cannabis preparations. Some 60 of these are classed together in the group called cannabinoids, and at least 6 of these are known to be psychoactive. They affect the human brain and nervous system, producing such mind changes as pleasure or anxiety.

The most important psychoactive chemical in cannabis is delta-9 tetrahydrocannabinol. The name is usually shortened to delta-9 THC or simply to THC. Delta-9 THC is not found anywhere else in nature. It has a complex chemical structure which is not like that of any other psychoactive drug.

Important, also, among the cannabinoids are cannabinol (CBN), cannabidiol (CBD), and cannabichromene (CBC). Still others are chemical cousins of delta-9 THC.

THE ELUSIVE WEED

Cannabis plants grown in different parts of the world are not exactly identical in chemical makeup. Jamaican cannabis, for example, is different from the Mexican plant in its proportions of delta-9 THC and CBN.

Not only that, but different parts of the plant contain different amounts of THC. The bract that covers the seeds may contain 10 percent THC or more, but the leaves might contain only 1 or 2 percent.

The THC content of the plant decreases in the following order: bracts, flowers, leaves, small stems, large stems, and roots and seeds. The seedless hybrid called sinsemilla maximizes the bracts. It is about ten times stronger than the ordinary varieties.

While cannabis is still growing in the field, its THC content can even vary with the time of day. Experiments have shown that a particular Mexican plant might contain 4.1 percent THC at eight o'clock in the morning, and 2.17 percent an hour later.

Any particular combination of the fifty or more different cannabinoids depends on temperature, water, soil conditions, and the variety of the plant itself.

Some of the mood-altering compounds are not active in the growing plant but emerge in the curing process or when burning activates them in the cigarette. Then, too, there are great differences in the chemical strength of each cannabis product: A marijuana cigarette may contain only 1 percent delta-9 THC, while hashish oil may contain as much as 65 percent or even more.

You can see that so many variables have often made results almost impossible to compare. Nowadays, therefore, experimenters begin by obtaining an exact analysis of all cannabinoids, as well as THC, present in the research material they will use.

METABOLISM—THE JOURNEY THROUGH THE BODY

To study what happens to cannabinoids once they have been smoked or eaten, scientists use a fascinating technique called tagging. It makes use of a radioactive form of chemical elements, usually carbon. The radiation involved is not strong enough to be harmful. Scientists replace one of the carbon or other atoms in THC with a radioactive atom. The THC behaves exactly the same as before, but now it has a tag attached to it. By using instruments for detecting radiation, researchers can follow the track of the tagged substance inside the body.

Studies with tagged THC show that when marijuana is smoked, only about 50 percent or less of the chemical enters the bloodstream through the lungs. When marijuana is eaten, as much as 95 percent enters the bloodstream through the digestive tract.

When delta-9 THC enters the body, the blood carries it to the liver. There it becomes transformed through a part of the digestive process called metabolism. The result of this process is a metabolite (product of metabolism) of THC that is a potent psychoactive chemical in its own right.

THC and its metabolite are not water soluble, which simply means that they can't be dissolved in water. But they are extremely soluble in fats. As they pass through all parts of the body, they encounter fatty tissue everywhere. They pass into the adrenal glands, the lungs, testes, ovaries, kidneys, and brain. They can enter every kind of cell and accumulate in every organ. Since they are not water soluble, the body cannot easily wash them out.

High levels of delta-9 THC and its metabolite remain for as long as seven days, especially in the brain. In one study of volunteers who had been given tagged THC, it was found that only 65 percent of the drug had been eliminated from the system at the end of one week. The human body seems to absorb delta-9 THC like a sponge. The drug permeates the body so completely that less than 1 percent can be found unchanged in eliminated wastes.

CANNABIS
AND
HEALTH

What are the exact effects of marijuana on the human mind and body?

The subject is clouded by emotion. Hardly any other drug has so many myths and misconceptions associated with it. Scientists working at world-famous laboratories have been accused by others of conducting poor research or interpreting results according to their own preconceived moral notions. In some cases it almost seems that the outcome of an experiment will depend on whether the researcher is for or against marijuana.

Still, there has been a great deal of competent and unbiased investigation all over the world. The evidence indicates that marijuana use is harmful. At the same time, though, as a medicine prescribed for certain illnesses, it may actually be beneficial.

How harmful is marijuana? There is no simple answer to this important question. Some of the most interesting studies have come up with controversial results and are inconclusive.

However, a new report, prepared in 1982 at the Institute of Medicine of the National Academy of Sciences, indicated that what little was known for certain about the effects of marijuana on human health justified serious national concern. Here, we will report both sides of the debate.

IMMUNITY RESPONSE

First of all, scientists have tried to learn how marijuana affects the body's ability to fight disease. Immunity to disease is the job of special white blood cells called lymphocytes. These cells specialize in fighting virus infections and destroying substances foreign to the body, such as cancer cells and organ transplants. When lymphocytes are challenged by such a foreign invader, they normally divide and grow very rapidly. This immunity response, as it is called, was tested by taking blood from the arms of a group of young marijuana smokers. The average amount smoked by the group was some three or four marijuana cigarettes a day. The lymphocytes were then isolated from the blood and tested by challenging the cells with special substances. It was found that the immunity response of smokers was 40 percent lower than that of nonsmokers. The smokers' weakened response was said to be similar to that of cancer patients.

Another series of experiments attempted to explain the lowered immunity by showing that the lymphocytes of marijuana smokers cannot produce sufficient DNA for proper cell division. DNA (deoxyribonucleic acid) is the basic chemical contained in our cells. It carries the basic genetic code which assures that every daughter cell is identical to its parent cell.

These results were challenged by a group of researchers who felt that the immunity response should be tested within the human body (*in vivo*) rather than in a test tube

A chimpanzee smokes a marijuana cigarette during a National Institutes of Health experiment to determine the drug's effects.

(*in vitro*). The response to a foreign irritant was checked in a number of marijuana smokers by rubbing DNA on their skin. In this test, the body's defense should result in reddening of the skin. All the responses were normal. It was concluded that marijuana smoking does not impair the immunity response in any way that can be detected by skin testing.

Recent studies show, however, that marijuana does produce a mild, transient suppression of the immune system which could produce an increase in infections among normal users. This could prove dangerous for people whose immune systems are already suppressed by illness.

CHROMOSOME DAMAGE

A second area of controversy involves the subject of chromosome damage in marijuana users. Most human cells contain 23 pairs of chromosomes. Chromosomes, which consist of long fibrous strands carrying genes, control the flow of genetic information during cell division and regulate the manufacture of important proteins within the cell itself. Abnormal chromosomes are known to lead to a higher incidence of birth defects and cancer. Studies were made of the chromosomes in the white blood cells of young marijuana smokers. Slides were prepared and scanned for any gaps or breaks or other signs of abnormal chromosomes. An increased chromosome breakage rate was found by one respected laboratory. Similar studies, however, performed in another laboratory by equally competent scientists, have so far failed to relate marijuana use to chromosome breakage.

BRAIN DAMAGE

The damage marijuana might cause to the brain has led to yet another controversy. Experiments were performed on a group of rhesus monkeys trained to smoke carefully controlled amounts of marijuana. Electrodes were implanted in the monkeys' brains, and the brain waves from important areas of the brain were recorded. A profound change was noted in the septal region. This is the site that controls alertness, awareness, and feelings of pleasure in humans. The changes were pronounced enough to resemble certain types of mental illness.

This research was criticized for being based on extremely large doses of marijuana. The doses given the monkeys were equivalent to doses resulting from smoking approximately 30 to 100 cigarettes a day.

More recently, however, two rhesus monkeys were trained to smoke the equivalent of only one marijuana cigarette a day. Even with this small dose, significant changes in brain structure were found. These included an enlargement of the synaptic cleft, the space across which nerve signals are transmitted from cell to cell. What effect this had on the actions of the monkeys was not determined.

RESPIRATORY DAMAGE

There is definite experimental evidence that marijuana smoke causes undesirable changes in lung cell structure. These changes are similar to those produced by tobacco smoke and resemble the abnormalities often found in precancerous tissue. Whether marijuana is more carcinogenic, or cancer-causing, than tobacco is not known, since it usually requires many years of exposure before the disease becomes apparent. What is of great interest, though, is the report that there are more carcinogenic chemicals in marijuana smoke than in tobacco smoke. More than 150 carcinogenic compounds have been identified in marijuana smoke. It has been estimated, therefore, that someone smoking five joints of marijuana per week will have a greater number of carcinogens in his or her lung tissues than someone smoking a pack a day of regular cigarettes. It should also be pointed out that like the tar from tobacco smoke, cannabis tar causes cancer when painted on mouse skin.

HORMONE DAMAGE

Another laboratory report on which there has been much debate deals with the apparent lowering of testosterone levels in men who are long-term marijuana smokers. Testosterone is a male hormone that stimulates the development of masculine characteristics, such as beard growth and lowering of the voice at puberty. The change in testosterone levels has been linked to a loss of sexual power and to a general lack of sexual desire. This is contrary to the popular ideas that marijuana makes people feel sexually stimulated. Experiments in other laboratories have failed to duplicate the hormone change exactly, and more research on this subject is being undertaken.

TOLERANCE

It has been shown that cannabis users develop tolerance to the drug. They have to use more and more to feel the high they are looking for. Reports from countries where there is a long history of cannabis use describe the enormous amounts of marijuana consumed. Smokers in the Middle East and Asia often end up using five or six times more than when they started.

MEDICAL USES

Before marijuana was declared illegal, physicians sometimes prescribed it for various ills. Today it is again under study for possible usefulness in medicine. It should be added, however, that medical use of cannabis in any form is permitted only in selected and closely supervised research projects.

Of some promise is the application of cannabis in the treatment of glaucoma. Glaucoma is an extremely serious eye disease caused by increased pressure of the fluid filling the eyeball. This increased pressure can damage the retina and cause blindness. It was observed that almost immediately on smoking marijuana, the pressure in the eyeball dropped and remained low for as long as five hours. Subsequent research has confirmed that this intraocular pressure (IOP) drop does indeed occur in most patients. There are still problems, though, in meeting general safety standards.

Marijuana may help people who suffer from asthma by opening up constricted air passages to the lungs. It seems to have a more persistent action than the usual medication. Unfortunately, inhaled marijuana smoke also irritates the lungs and throat. Marijuana in spray form is under consideration.

Finally, marijuana may prove to be of aid in reducing the side effects of certain kinds of cancer treatment. In one common form of cancer therapy, patients are given powerful drugs in the hope that these will destroy the malignant (cancer) cells. One of the undesirable side effects of the treatment is that it produces nausea and vomiting. Recent studies have indicated that delta-9 THC helps to reduce these symptoms. It also helps cancer patients to feel less depressed and to eat with a better appetite.

Other applications are being investigated. One day marijuana may be used to relieve pain, and to control convulsions in epileptic patients.

Marijuana is thought to be promising as a medical drug because it is surprisingly nontoxic. It can be given to patients in large doses without being deadly. The hope is that humanity will be able to benefit from cannabis and to avoid its noxious effects.

MENTAL HEALTH

Frequent marijuana use is now generally considered harmful to mental health, particularly in young people. It seems to block the emotional transition from childhood to adulthood, and to interfere with maturing. This was the consensus of most doctors and psychiatrists who met in a work group at the National Institute on Drug Abuse in 1981. Again and again these experts spoke of young marijuana users whose school work had declined, who felt estranged from their families, who lost interest in traditional tasks and values, and who felt lonely and suspicious.

The experience of certain American high school seniors bears this out. In a confidential survey conducted nationwide in 1979 and 1980, between 34 and 42 percent of high school students who used marijuana daily reported a loss of energy and of interest in other activities. They also said their relations with their parents had deteriorated and that their performance at school had dropped noticeably.

LOTOS EATERS

In the ancient Greek poem, the *Odyssey*, we read about an island people called the Lotos Eaters. When Odysseus and his men stopped at the island on their long, weary way home after the Trojan War, the Lotos Eaters offered the sailors some of their flowering food. Those who tasted it forgot their families and the waiting ship. They only wanted to stay on the island, daydreaming instead of continuing their journey.

We can't be sure that the flowering food in the story was marijuana. But the sailors' reaction certainly resembles that described by many marijuana users. Psychologists have given the name "amotivational syndrome" to this state of mind. The term implies a loss of desire to cope with difficulties or to act and move forward in life.

AN EXPERT OPINION

To find out more about the effects of marijuana on the minds of young users, we spoke with Mr. John Imhof, a distinguished social worker who concerns himself chiefly with drug problems and youth. Mr. Imhof directs the Drug Treatment and Education Center of North Shore University Hospital in Manhasset, New York. He is also editor in chief of the *Journal of Substance Abuse Treatment.*

We sat with Mr. Imhof in his pleasant office while he talked about young people who have been hurt by drugs.

"If scientists all over the world got together," he began, "and tried to devise a chemical substance that could effectively interfere with, and halt, and block, adolescent development, they couldn't come up with a more effective agent than marijuana. The impact it has on the emotions and psychological development of youngsters is profound. In effect, the use of marijuana begins to halt the maturational process."

We asked how he had been able to observe this arrested development.

"We see many patients come into our center at the average age of twenty-three or twenty-four," Mr. Imhof said. "By that time their drug use may have progressed to cocaine or heroin or barbiturates. On the form they fill out, they usually list their first use of marijuana at the age of twelve or thirteen. Now, when we begin talking with these patients in therapy, they're still twelve-year-olds, thirteen-year-olds. You can see the cessation of emotional development at the age at which they began regular, compulsive drug use.

"Think of it," he went on. "We have in our country a chemical agent that is effectively interfering with the development of the next generation and the generation after that—the generation that will be in power in our society one day."

Did Mr. Imhof believe every single experience of marijuana must have such serious consequences? Not necessarily. Actually, he sees drug use as a symptom of an underlying emotional difficulty.

"I'm not talking about the kid who tries it once or twice and never goes back. The problem develops in the youngster who takes the drug and experiences from it a feeling of well-being or euphoria he or she gets nowhere else. The problem develops in the kid who's using the chemical to fill a void.

"When we talk to young people who come to our center we often find they have tremendous anxiety. They turn to marijuana, as some people do to alcohol, as an anti-anxiety medication. Unfortunately, a serious by-product of marijuana is depression, and if a young person tends toward depression in the first place the use of marijuana will intensify it."

Mr. Imhof also noted that instead of helping boys and girls relate to other people, marijuana increases a tendency to put up an emotional barrier between themselves and others. He calls it a sort of invisible shield that prevents a user from making contact with the outside world.

SORTING THINGS OUT

One thing became clear in our talk with Mr. Imhof. Turning to marijuana for relief from oppressive feelings is a sure way not to solve one's problems. It's better to try working them out. Emotional hurts are as serious as physical ones and need experienced help. If help from parents hasn't been a success, a young person who's feeling unbearably sad, anxious, or upset can turn to a school advisor, a friendly teacher, a clergyman, or a counselor in a mental health center.

Teenage girls talk about their problems with a counselor at a drug treatment center.

Most communities now have their own drug counseling and treatment centers. The professionals who work there will not pick up the phone and call parents the minute a youngster walks in for help. As a rule, though, anyone under eighteen who wants to start regular treatments needs parental consent.

SAYING NO

Today, just about every young person is subject to being offered a drug such as marijuana. At one time or another, the moment may come when someone says, "Here, have some. Try it!"—under circumstances that make it difficult or embarrassing to refuse.

It takes courage to reply, "No thanks." In fact, it takes quite an act of self-assertion. But in Mr. Imhof's opinion, "the kid who says, 'No—I don't need it, I don't want it,' deserves a lot of praise. He or she is really the hero of the situation."

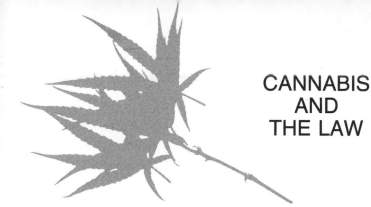

CANNABIS
AND
THE LAW

During the early years of this century, Americans could buy every sort of drug at the local pharmacy. Some manufacturers of patent medicines even sold narcotics mixed in syrup or alcohol as remedies for a long list of illnesses. People who bought the medicines often became seriously addicted. Slowly, the public awakened to the dangers of habit-forming drugs. In Britain an act was introduced which prohibited the sale of drugs without a doctor's prescription.

In 1914, the U.S. Congress passed the Harrison Narcotics Act. The act controlled substances such as opium and cocaine. They were to be available only as carefully prescribed drugs. Marijuana, though, was almost unknown to the American public at that time. It was not classified as a narcotic and was not mentioned in the new law.

Over the years, however, marijuana became enough of a local nuisance to be outlawed in one American state after another. From the states bordering Mexico, and from Louisiana, banning of the weed moved north and east. By 1930, each state had its own antidrug law and sixteen mentioned marijuana in particular. In Britain the 1925 Dangerous Drugs Act added marijuana to the list of narcotics banned from import/export production and dealings.

As yet, marijuana was not included in the federal drug regulations. But in 1930 the Federal Bureau of Narcotics was created. Its chief, Harry J. Anslinger, was especially concerned with the dangers of what he called "the killer weed." He ran a strong campaign against it in newspapers and magazines.

Marijuana received lots of publicity. In New York City, police officers were taught how to recognize the weed and destroy it. It had been growing here and there, unnoticed, all along. One of these wild hemp fields, near the Brooklyn Bridge, was uprooted in 1934.

THE MARIJUANA TAX ACT

Commissioner Anslinger succeeded in his campaign. In 1937 Congress passed the Marijuana Tax Act. It reinforced the local state laws already in effect. The tax act provided that sale of marijuana for research or medical use be taxed $1.00 per ounce (28.4 g), and that sale for any other purpose be taxed $100.00 per ounce. The minimum penalty for not paying the tax was a $2,000 fine, and the maximum was five years in prison. In Britain the maximum penalty was ten years' imprisonment.

As yet, the general public had little personal acquaintance with marijuana. It belonged to the world of jazz clubs and waterfront bars. A study undertaken in New York City under Mayor Fiorello H. La Guardia shows that in the years between 1938 and 1944, marijuana smoking was practically unknown among the city's teenagers.

THE AGE OF DRUG ABUSE

During the World War II years—the 1940s—the U.S. Federal Bureau of Narcotics really seemed to have stopped the marijuana habit from spreading. Suddenly, though, in the 1950s, drug abuse became a noticeable problem. In the big cities, thousands of young people fell victim to the addictive and deadly narcotic heroin. In suburbs, in small towns, and on college campuses, youngsters were drawn into trying drugs such as LSD and the legally produced amphetamines, barbiturates, and tranquilizers.

Soon, legislators feared that marijuana might be only an entry-level drug—a stepping-stone leading people on to hard narcotics. To control this menace, penalties for possession and use of cannabis were raised several times. The Narcotics Control Act of 1956 made simple possession enough evidence of guilt to convict. It imposed a minimum sentence of two years in prison for a first offense. It made selling by an adult to a juvenile punishable by a minimum prison sentence of ten years. Possession of marijuana was classified as a felony. That placed it in the same class of crime as armed bank robbery.

New powers were granted to agents of the U.S. bureaus of Narcotics and of Customs. They were allowed to carry firearms. Police departments put great effort into arresting drug users. Those were the years of the "drug bust," when police searched college dormitories before dawn and raided parties in private homes.

Even so, cannabis use kept on rising. In the United States alone, there were 18,815 state and local arrests in 1965. In 1971, there were 225,828. By the mid-1970s, the number had risen to about 500,000. Clearly, threats of severe prison sentences and large fines had done little to discourage marijuana use.

THE CONTROLLED SUBSTANCES ACT

In 1970, a new federal law—the Comprehensive Drug Abuse Prevention and Control Act—went into effect. This law, often called the Controlled Substances Act, classified the various legal and illegal drugs in groups and assigned penalties for violations in each group. Marijuana was classified not as a narcotic—a drug that can make the user lose consciousness—but as a hallucinogen, a drug that alters the user's senses or perceptions. Most important of all, the act removed the minimum sentence and reduced possession of a small quantity of marijuana from a felony to a misdemeanor—a much lighter offense.

To help the different states in making their drug laws conform to each other as well as to federal standards, the National Conference of Commissioners on Uniform State Laws approved a Uniform Controlled Substances Act (1970). The act recommends that the states reduce possession of 1 ounce (28.4 g) or less of cannabis for one's own use to a misdemeanor. The change makes it possible for first offenders to be put on probation rather than in prison. If they are under twenty-one, they may request to have their criminal record erased. Most of the states have adopted the Uniform Act.

THE DRUG ENFORCEMENT ADMINISTRATION

In 1973, the president of the United States reorganized the agencies that had been responsible for drug enforcement. The former Bureau of Narcotics and Dangerous Drugs, the Office for Drug Abuse Law Enforcement, the Office of National Narcotics Intelligence, the drug-related branches of the Bureau of Customs and of the Office of Science and Technology—all these were now merged in one new central organization, the Drug Enforcement Administration.

Working within the Department of Justice, the Drug Enforcement Administration performs many tasks. It concerns itself with every aspect of drug policy enforcement. It searches out illegal supplies and brings offenders to trial.

It collects scientific data and makes new information available to the public. It helps train law enforcement officers; it cooperates with state and local drug enforcement efforts; and it takes part in worldwide drug control programs.

DECRIMINALIZATION

Law enforcement is expensive. In the 1970s some $6 billion were spent each year on the arrest and prosecution of marijuana offenders. Many experts, including police chiefs in major cities, thought this a high price to pay for a relatively small impact on cannabis trafficking. They tended to agree that law enforcement efforts must concentrate on more serious crimes, and sided with widespread public opinion that using pot should be classified as a lighter offense than a felony.

Three states—Alaska, Maine, and Oregon—led the way in decriminalizing possession of small amounts of cannabis for personal use. In Oregon, for example, a user caught in possession of pot was now handed a citation very much like a traffic ticket and made to pay a fine. A follow-up study showed that the citizens of Oregon were satisfied with the change. At the same time, though, it has been pointed out that after decriminalization the number of users in the eighteen- to twenty-nine-year-old age group increased from 46 percent to 62 percent. Another effect seems to have been that law officials in Oregon began to seize greater quantities of marijuana than ever before. All the same, one state after another has followed suit in decriminalizing possession of small amounts of marijuana for personal use.

THE CASE OF T.L.O.

It's important to keep in mind that decriminalization is not the same thing as legalization. This is borne out by the case of a New Jersey public high school student, a young girl identified in court records only as T.L.O.

The case began in 1980, when a school official saw the student smoking, searched her purse, and found evidence that she was using and selling marijuana. She was turned over to the police and sentenced as a delinquent in juvenile court. Later, though, the New Jersey Supreme Court reversed the judgment under the Fourteenth Amendment of the federal Constitution, which prohibits unreasonable searches by state officers. The evidence was declared inadmissible because it was not obtained on "probable cause" for thinking that a violation of law had occurred.

In turn, the state of New Jersey contested this decision on behalf of its public school officials. At last, early in 1985, the U.S. Supreme Court ruled 6 to 3 that public school officials and teachers may search a student if there are reasonable grounds for thinking the search will reveal a violation of the law or of school rules.

Reporters asked seniors at the school "T.L.O." had attended how they reacted to this important decision. Although many of them felt strongly about keeping purses and pockets private territory, they did agree that students should not be permitted to bring things like drugs or weapons into schools. The consensus was that a search may sometimes be warranted, but only if school officials have a strong and reasonable suspicion that a student is doing something unlawful.

DRUGS AND TRAVEL

Americans journeying abroad are often unaware that other countries have even stricter penalties for using and selling marijuana than the United States. Right now, many Americans who ignored local marijuana laws are sitting out prison terms in foreign jails from Nigeria to Mexico. In

Britain, for instance, the maximum penalty for possession of marijuana is five years' imprisonment and an unlimited fine. Supply and cultivation of the drug can carry a maximum penalty of fourteen years' imprisonment and a fine. The number of arrests in Britain had passed the 10,000 mark in 1980.

In 1961 the United States entered an international drug policy agreement with 108 other nations. This so-called Single Convention Treaty requires that the countries involved restrict and control the use of marijuana and other drugs, and gradually eliminate all drug crops grown on their territories. Even countries where marijuana was formerly in public use have begun educating their people as to its possible effects and are tightening their drug laws.

It is interesting that some parts of the world are beginning to criminalize an age-old habit, while the United States, where the habit is recent, has moved towards its decriminalization.

AN AVALANCHE
OF DRUGS

You may wonder how so many cannabis users manage to supply their habit. Smugglers bring some $5 billion worth of marijuana into the United States each year. Like other illegal drugs, marijuana crosses the borders by land, air, and sea. It travels from countries such as Colombia, Jamaica, and Mexico by cars, trucks, yachts, and fishing boats. It moves in big cargo planes that swoop down at night on improvised runways in the forest. In one case, a shipment went in a surplus B–25 bomber. The plane crashed into a hillside in Georgia, killing its pilots and dumping about 2 tons (1.8 t) of marijuana into a field.

Often, customs officials arrive to find only an empty aircraft. When profits are as large as $1.5 million for a 5-ton

(4.5 t) haul, smugglers can afford to abandon a $40,000 plane.

On the whole, though, because the cargo is bulky, ships are the most convenient way to run marijuana. Sometimes the smugglers land as far north as Boston, Massachusetts, and the coast of Maine. Recently, a freighter spotted off the New England coast was found to carry 33 tons (30 t) of marijuana under a false bottom in its hold. Marijuana is smuggled into the United Kingdom by similar means.

To hold back this flood of drugs is the job of the United States Customs Service. The Customs Service has hired hundreds of new enforcement officers and bought new boats, planes, and other expensive equipment. But even though drug seizures have increased over a hundredfold within two or three years; the tonnage of drugs shipped in has risen even higher. In 1985, Customs estimated that its program was catching about 1 of every 100 drug-smuggling airplanes and about 6 of every hundred boats.

GOING TO THE ROOTS

The U.S. border is so long that it may never be totally under control. For this reason, the government began, in the late 1970s, to try getting directly at the roots of the drug supply. With the help of the countries concerned—mainly Mexico, Colombia, and Jamaica—the United States supervised crop destruction and tried to help farmers switch over to other kinds of produce.

The campaign started in Mexico, where helicopter pilots sprayed the weed-killer paraquat across marijuana fields.

Authorities in New York City unload bales of marijuana seized from a sailboat thirty miles east of Bermuda.

Later, after farmers complained of health problems and damage to nearby food crops, another, safer weed-killer was substituted.

Crop eradication was partly successful. But when the Mexican cannabis supply began to dwindle, growers in the jungles of Colombia took over and became number-one suppliers in the market. As for substitute crops, small growers seldom found them worth their labor. Marijuana flourishes more easily than most vegetables and sells for a higher price. There was no end to the drug supply.

In 1984, the U.S. government passed an amendment to the foreign aid bill. It required Congress to stop giving financial help to countries where drugs are cultivated unless their governments take "adequate steps" to reduce all aspects of drug trafficking. Although the countries concerned all initiated anti-drug campaigns, they still faced the same difficulties we have at home. Controlling drug cultivation and traffic is tricky and costly. It is also dangerous. Back in 1983 a Colombia minister of justice led a serious crackdown on the drug trade, and was killed in the street by gunmen.

BACKYARD CULTIVATION

It seems that whenever officials manage to suppress one area of drug commerce, it rears up somewhere else. When crop eradication and criminal prosecution abroad met with some success, imported marijuana became scarcer and more expensive. This did not slow down trade, however. On the contrary. Scarcity encouraged American domestic production, which soon flourished into a major, illegal agricultural business.

By 1985, half of all marijuana consumed in the United States was estimated to be grown there. In the state of

Florida, its sale was said to exceed that of oranges in value. Today it is known to be an important undercover part of the economy in many states, even as far north as New York, Vermont, and New Hampshire. Some plantings are on private land, and may be protected by masked men carrying rifles. Others are hidden deep in the wilderness of national forests and state parks.

"Garden patch" cultivators on park lands have become a threat to incautious visitors. In some cases they have shot at hikers, beaten them up or set booby traps for them. Police have even reported murders related to intrusion on pot patches in California's redwood forests.

Patch gardeners also tend to damage public lands by fires, tree-cutting, pesticides, and fertilizers. The Forest Service has had to close certain areas temporarily, to protect the public from armed marijuana growers and such devices as trip wires triggering shotguns.

Fighting outlaw marijuana farmers is not as easy as it might seem. Armed searches of private grounds are unconstitutional. On public lands, officers of the Drug Enforcement Administration have to proceed as in a jungle war. They descend, armed, from spotter planes and helicopters, burn or spray the harvest they find, make arrests, and seize guns and vehicles. Growers have countered by military camouflage.

Yet law enforcement has been tough enough on patch gardeners to drive some of them indoors. The new variety of cannabis called sinsemilla grows well under hothouse conditions. Its seedless buds are far more potent than the old varieties, so a grower needs fewer plants to make a hefty profit. Sinsemilla flourishes in hiding, where one would never suspect it—in sheds, attics, warehouses, and garages. It grows under artificial light, and sometimes even hydroponically, in water tanks instead of soil.

*Burning marijuana crops during a nationwide
search-and-destroy operation in 1985.
Federal agents work with state and local police
to discourage illegal marijuana farming.*

SHOULD MARIJUANA
BE LEGAL?

Our current drug situation reminds many observers of Prohibition—the period in U.S. history when alcoholic drinks were outlawed. Instead of decreasing the demand for liquor, Prohibition surrounded drinking with an air of secrecy and daring that added to its prestige. Bootleggers and gangsters took over the liquor business and criminals made fortunes on it. After thirteen unsuccessful years, Prohibition was repealed in 1933.

Similarly today, the undercover quality of drug traffic tends to glamorize it. It also fosters crime, promotes a widening circle of users, and monopolizes the attention of law enforcement agencies. It is a billion-dollar industry that never pays a penny in taxes, bringing the government only expenses instead of revenues.

Wouldn't it be better to legalize a drug such as marijuana, some people ask? It could be packaged with a warning label, restricted to adult use, and heavily taxed. Having it legally available might reduce part of its appeal and put the small-time trafficker out of business. (The big-timer, of course, might even benefit from legalization. It would turn him from a criminal into a respectable entrepreneur overnight.)

Arnold Trebach, director of the Institute on Drugs, Crime and Justice at American University in Washington, endorses legalization. He believes that no matter how much we prosecute the traffickers, they will get around any enforcement strategy. Marijuana should be sold legally and taxed. The revenue should be devoted to intensive drug-abuse treatment and education programs.

On the other hand, Dr. William Pollin at the National Institute on Drug Abuse thinks legalization could only end in disaster. He points out how many million Americans abuse tobacco and alcohol even though public education campaigns have shown the harm caused by these legally available substances.

We asked Mr. Imhof—the social worker whom you met earlier—what he thought of legalizing marijuana.

"Alcohol is legal," Mr. Imhof said, shaking his head, "and look at the casualties! Twelve million alcoholics in this country! Thirty thousand people dying on the roads due to alcohol-induced traffic accidents every year! Untold billions of dollars lost in income, work, and productivity!"

No. Mr. Imhof doesn't think legalization is a good solution to our problem. And come to think of it, wouldn't legalizing marijuana be like saying "Go ahead! It's OK to help yourself"? Wouldn't a legitimate marijuana industry run advertising and sales campaigns? Wouldn't companies compete in trying to start an increasing number of users on the habit? And wouldn't age restrictions continue to make marijuana tempting to youngsters? Aren't tobacco and alcohol enough, and do we really want to add another harmful substance to the open market?

It's interesting that many young people today are turning against legalization. In 1977, 52.9 percent of college students questioned in the nationwide annual survey of freshman attitudes backed legalization of marijuana. But by 1983 the number had dropped to 25.7 percent, and by 1984 it was down to 22.9 percent. These students seem to agree that drugs, being both seductive and harmful, must be fought on many fronts at once. Just the simple fact that marijuana is illegal does keep many people away from it.

One thing is certain, though. The law alone will never be enough to give us a drug-free society. Because of the many things we are learning about drugs, people will need to be wiser in their decisions than ever before. Indeed, drugs—both legal and illegal—pose one of the most important health and social questions of our time.

GLOSSARY

Amotivational syndrome. A state of mind combining loss of energy and lack of interest in coping with the demands of normal living. Often seems to result from frequent marijuana use.

Angel Dust. See phencyclidine (PCP).

Bhang. A mild form of marijuana used in India, often as medicine.

Cannabidiol (CBD). A constituent of marijuana. One of the compounds that make up the chemical family known as cannabinoids.

Cannabinoids. A general term for the family of similar chemical compounds, all containing 21 carbon atoms, found in the marijuana plant.

Cannabinol (CBN). A major cannabinoid found in cannabis.

Cannabis. A general term for any of the various preparations of the marijuana plant. Marijuana, hashish, and tetrahydrocannabinol (THC) are examples of different forms or compounds of cannabis.

Cannabis sativa. Also known as hemp. It is a herbaceous annual plant that readily grows in temperate climates. Preparations made from the plant may contain 420 different compounds; of these, 61 have been identified as cannabinoids, many of which possess some biological activity.

Delta-9 THC. One of the principal constituents of the group of cannabinoids known as tetrahydrocannabinol. In the

United States, the delta-9 THC content in marijuana ranges from trace amounts to about 6 percent.

Ganja. Originally the Hindi name for marijuana. Now commonly used in the West Indies.

Hashish. A strong concentrate of marijuana made from resins of the female flower.

Marijuana. A general term for crude preparations obtained from the plant *Cannabis sativa.* Usually a mixture of crushed leaves, twigs, seeds, and sometimes the flower of the plant.

Phencyclidine (PCP). An animal tranquilizer also known as "angel dust." Sometimes sold under the name of "T," through a confusion with the marijuana-derivative THC. Used as an additive to marijuana.

Psychoactive. Having a mind-altering effect.

Sinsemilla. A seedless hybrid strain of marijuana that is more potent than ordinary varieties and grows well in North America. Originally grown in California.

Tetrahydrocannabinol (THC). One of the major groups of cannabinoids. Delta-9 THC is the principal active constituent in natural cannabis preparations.

ORGANIZATIONS TO CONSULT ABOUT MARIJUANA

American Council for Drug Education
6193 Executive Blvd., Rockville, MD 20852
(301) 984–5700
The Council is staffed by doctors, psychiatrists, clergy, and other professionals and concerned individuals. It disseminates information on marijuana, cocaine, and other psychoactive drugs. It offers information kits, conducts conferences and seminars, publishes a quarterly newsletter, and produces AV materials such as films, radio and television programs, and videotapes.

Center for the Study of Drug Policy
2035 P Street NW #401, Washington, DC 20036
(202) 331–7363
The Center gathers data, mainly about marijuana, its use and misuse. It observes medical findings, monitors public policy, and maintains a library and statistics. It is affiliated with the National Organization for the Reform of Marijuana Laws (NORML).

Potsmokers Anonymous
316 East Third Street, New York, NY 10009
(212) 254–1777
This organization offers a 9-week course for people who want to stop smoking marijuana. In addition, Potsmokers Anonymous provides public education lectures and presentations, and maintains a library for staff members.

FOR
FURTHER
READING

Berger, Gilda. *Addiction: Its Causes, Problems and Treatment.* New York: Franklin Watts, 1982.

Jackson, Bruce, and Jackson, Michael. *Doing Drugs.* New York: St. Martin's/Marek, 1983.

National Institute on Drug Abuse Research. *Adolescent Marijuana Abusers and Their Families.* Monograph no. 40, 1981. For sale by the Superintendent of Documents, Government Printing Office, Washington, DC 20402.

U.S. Department of Health and Human Services. *Marijuana and Youth.* Publication no. (ADM) 82–1186; 1982. For sale by the Superintendent of Documents, Government Printing Office, Washington, DC 20402.

Woods, Geraldine. *Drug Use and Drug Abuse.* New York: Franklin Watts, 1986.

INDEX